ENGLISH COSTUME OF THE EARLY MIDDLE AGES

1250

English Costume

of the

Early Middle Ages

The Tenth to the Thirteenth Centuries

Drawn and Described by
Iris Brooke

A. & C. Black, Ltd
4, 5 & 6 Soho Square, London, W.1

FIRST PUBLISHED 1936
REPRINTED 1948 AND 1956

MADE IN GREAT BRITAIN

FOREWORD

A S with the other books in this series, dealing with later costume, this must be taken only as a reasonably comprehensive guide to dress worn in this country from the 10th to the 13th century. Positive accuracy is clearly impossible in the reconstruction of clothes worn over one thousand years ago. It will be obvious that it is not practicable to arrange the groups of drawings in this book into short periods of years, as in the other books in this series; the drawings have therefore been arranged as accurately as possible in their probable sequence in four sections covering the four centuries with which the book is concerned.

Anglo-Saxon England was, it must be remembered, populated by a restless, warlike, and scattered people, perpetually harried by opposing forces, and clothes were little more than a necessary defence against the elements, the chief factor in dress being warmth and utility. It was not until well after the Conquest that costume became, in addition, a method of self-expression.

The Anglo-Saxon Chronicle and most of the later records of the period are concerned only with details of wars and battles, plagues and famines, harvests and even weather conditions, and, with almost the solitary exception of Matthew Paris, the chroniclers devote little or no space to clothes. The most useful source of information is to be found in the illuminated religious manuscripts in the British Museum and in numerous other libraries in this country and abroad; for the student with limited time at his disposal the British Museum has an excellent collection of originals and reproductions of practically all the most important contemporary works.

The 11th, 12th, and 13th centuries yield several contemporary ivories and chessmen, delicately carved and of exquisite workmanship, and these, together with the effigies and other relief carvings, are of far more technical value than any drawing, as they show in detail the line and flow of the draperies which played such an important part in the costume of that time. Indeed, during the 12th and 13th centuries the effigies had a naturalness that is not to be found in the more mannered sculptures of a later date.

The Bayeux Tapestry, of course, is also a useful source of pictorial information, but here again we must face the problem of lack of authentic dated records. In all probability this work was stretched over a great many years, and it is reasonable to surmise that it was not finished until at least a century after the Norman Conquest.

Alfred the Great, Canute, William the Conqueror, and Richard Cœur de Lion appear in these pages, and their costumes, simple in cut and design, are at once dignified and graceful, and form a striking contrast to the elaborate and fantastic costume of the later Middle Ages.

I. B.

ENGLISH COSTUME
OF
THE EARLY MIDDLE AGES

900—1000

ALTHOUGH the period with which this book is concerned begins with the tenth century, there were so few changes of costume during the Anglo-Saxon period that the first pages of drawings might equally apply to the two previous centuries.

From the scanty references to costume in the Anglo-Saxon Chronicle and other contemporary sources, it is evident that interest in costume was confined to its suitability as a covering and protection for the body. The only direction in which development was made was in the materials used, and great strides were made in weaving flax, wool, and even a little silk into fine materials. At this time all classes wore garments of practically the same type, and distinctions of rank were indicated by the richness of the material and the costliness of the personal decoration rather than by the form of the garments.

Ladies of high position spent much time in carding wool, spinning, and working with the needle. Embroidery was carried out in gold, silver, and coloured threads of silk and wool, and sometimes set with jewels. Many of the embroideries were of Byzantine design, an influence partly due to the introduction of a number of Greek weavers into the country.

9 0 0—1 0 0 0 (*continued*)

Women's garments at this time consisted of a loose outer
gown or super tunic, cut fairly full and with wide sleeves
reaching just below the elbow, but sometimes longer and
turned back.   Worn without a girdle, the gown was usually
ankle-length but hitched up at the sides or front to about
knee-length.   Under this outer gown was worn another
gown, long and full with sleeves tight at the wrist.   Beneath
this was worn another garment of the same shape, and the
Anglo-Saxon name for this undermost garment was " smock."
The cloaks worn by women were semicircular in shape and
arranged so that the back portion was considerably longer
than the front.

For the most part the colours of both men's and women's
garments were the natural colours of the homespun materials,
subdued colours such as greys and browns and bright blues,
greens, and reds.

Ecclesiastical costume is not dealt with in this book, but
as examples of embroidered garments are so few the designs
on the priest's garments on the page facing are particularly
interesting.

9 0 0—1 0 0 0 (*continued*)

The usual foundation garment for men was cut on lines similar to modern pyjama trousers, and was known by the Anglo-Saxons as " bracco," and the Normans as " braies." Over the braies were worn cross-garterings, or the legs were bound from knee to ankle with leather thongs. These leg-bindings were very convenient for outdoor workers, and in a somewhat modified form have persisted through the centuries and are still worn by farm workers in some parts of the country to-day. Many of the people went barefoot with only their ankles bound.

During the tenth century few varieties of head-dress were worn by men except the helmet-shaped hat with a point at the top called a " Phrygian cap," the close-fitting cap and the plain gold coronet worn by people of rank. These three types of head-dress are illustrated on the opposite page.

Women's heads were always covered except in the cases of very young girls and slaves. Throughout this early period women's head-dresses were very simple and little variety can be found in the arrangement of the head-veil, the French name for which was " couvrechef " and the Anglo-Saxon " heafods-rægel " or head-rail. The first of the three examples illustrated is an arrangement for a very light fabric, as the weight of a heavy material would pull the loosely arranged folds off the head. The second head-dress shows a couvrechef of a smaller piece of material, with one end brought round and flung over the opposite shoulder. The last example was the most general manner of head-covering. Clasped beneath the chin with a brooch, it often hung in folds almost to the length of the gown itself, serving the double purpose of head-dress and cloak. This idea was often adopted by the men in colder weather, and their cloaks which were usually fastened at the shoulder were swung round so that the fastening was in front, and the cloak could then be easily drawn up over the head.

900—1000 *(continued)*

In addition to the foundation garment, the costume of an ordinary man consisted of a shirt, tunic, and cloak. The tunic was knee-length and belted or fastened tight at the waist. It was drawn on over the head and the neck opening was often fastened with a brooch. The tunics varied little except in the sleeves, which were sometimes close-fitting, cut several inches longer than the arm and pushed up over the wrist so that a corrugated effect was formed below the elbow. In other cases the sleeves were quite loose and reached only half-way down the forearm, disclosing the tightly-fitting shirt beneath. The upper classes wore bands of embroidery at the wrist or hem.

Cloaks were worn by all classes, and in shape were square, oblong, or semicircular, and similar to those worn by the women.

9 0 0 — 1 0 0 0 (*continued*)

The whole of the Anglo-Saxon period is one of struggle
and unrest, and their preoccupation with war and conquest
and the primitive state of their civilization explain the reasons
for the slow development of costume. The tribes of Angles,
Saxons, and Jutes in various parts of the country fought
continually amongst themselves for supremacy. Eventually
seven separate kingdoms emerged, but the struggle continued
and out of these seven, three gained supremacy—Northum-
bria, Mercia, and Wessex, and in turn they exercised supremacy over each other. Under the pressure of the invasion
from the North, Wessex gained a lasting dominion over the
country, but although strong enough to check the invaders,
the Danes were too strong to be expelled. At first the
object of the Danes was plunder, but towards the middle of
the ninth century their aim became settlement. Under
Alfred a compromise was reached and the Danes agreed to
remain within a specified part of the country known as the
Danelaw. It was recaptured by Alfred's descendants, and
England became a more united country.

Towards the end of the tenth century, however, Danish
attacks recommenced, and after a period of misery and
desolation under Ethelred the Unready, early in the eleventh
century the country was finally captured by Canute, who
was also king of Denmark and later of Norway, too. Under
Canute's rule peace came to the country. Trade and com-
merce flourished not only between England and the king's
Scandinavian dominions, but with the Mediterranean lands
where the Danes and Norwegians had already penetrated.

Traders returned with the products of a more advanced
civilization, silks and finely woven cloth, gems and costly
metals and elaborate leather work, and from this time begins
the slow but gradual development of costume into the
fantastic raiment of the later Middle Ages.

1000—1100

THE figures on the page facing are taken from a drawing representing King Canute and his Queen, reputed to have been executed sometime between 1016 and 1020. There are one or two interesting innovations to note. The sleeves of the Queen's gown do not hang loose at the wrist, but are gathered in by a tight band, and the couvrechef is worn over a coronet. This custom seems to be confined to the early part of the eleventh century, although a later example may be seen in the figure on page 27, the date of which is approximately 1070.

The comparatively neat cut of the king's hair and beard shows a distinct advance on examples in earlier drawings. The beard and moustache are both well-trimmed and shaped, and the hair is cut short on the forehead and is allowed to curl slightly at the back. The hose are gartered at the top with a band of embroidery and cross-garterings are dispensed with. Another innovation is the ring on the cloak ; although not in use it seems quite clear that the two ends of the cloak were drawn through it, fastening the cloak at any desired height. Throughout this period swords were only worn on formal occasions and in times of war, and not as at a later date as an ornament.

I O O O—I I O O (*continued*)

The first figure on the opposite page shows the hose drawn up to the knee with a garter or band of embroidery at the top. The hose were of a loosely woven material and were pulled over the braies, which were made of white or coloured linen and reached the ankle. Cross-garterings and the puttee-like bindings were still worn during the first half of the century, but were not seen so much at the Conquest.

Shoes were a little more ornamental than previously, and as time went on were cut higher at the ankle until towards the end of the century they were more like a boot with a turned-down top. They were usually slit down the side or front and tied at the top or fastened with a buckle or brooch. The Anglo-Saxons had long understood the tanner's art, and a variety of leather was available for shoes. Undressed leather was used for rougher shoes, and dressed leather, often coloured and gilded, for the shoes of the wealthy. Cloth and felt were also used for shoes, and often embroidered and ornamented.

It will be seen that leg-wear consisted of three distinct items—the braies, the hose, and the shoes or boots. Short hose, made of leather or other material, were often worn over the hose, sometimes with and sometimes without shoes.

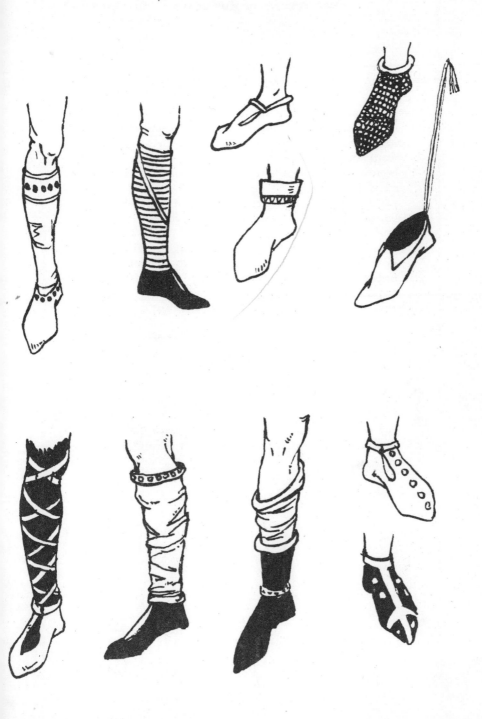

I O O O—I I O O (*continued*)

As garments at this time had no pockets, personal possessions such as keys, purses, and knives and daggers were
suspended from the belt or girdle. Belts were sometimes
worn under the tunic, and in the tight-fitting tunic at the
bottom of the opposite page the sides have been slit to
allow easy access, although as often the skirts of the tunic
were cut full this was not necessary. If the belt was worn
outside, the tunic was drawn up and allowed to flop over,
thus hiding the belt itself.

In some tunics of this time, as on page 31, there is a band
of embroidery at the waist or above it. This is part of the
ornamentation of the gown similar to the bands of embroidery at the neck and elbow and should not be confused
with the belt. In this example the belt was worn under the
tunic. The garments worn by both men and women at
this time were extremely simple in cut and design. The lower
half of the man's garment was practically a half-circle, so
that the skirt of the tunic was very full, and if the tunic was
long it was almost pleated in its fullness. The women's
tunics were not cut on such a generous scale, but their
fullness gave little scope for displaying the figure. It was
not until the twelfth century that women's garments began
to develop into the revealing garments of later periods.

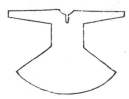

I O O O—I I O O (*continued*)

It was during the second half of the eleventh century that linings to gowns and cloaks were first used to any extent. The linings were usually of a contrasting colour, although the wealthy occasionally used fur. Borders of embroidery or appliqued designs were more popular than earlier in the century and for the most part followed simple geometrical designs.

Cloaks were worn in a variety of ways, and sometimes, as on the page facing, after the Roman manner. These cloaks were cut in a circular pattern ; some were simply a half-circle of material with a large ring sewn at one side of the neck through which the other side of the cloak was pulled, as in the first drawing on page 29.   They were cut in a variety of lengths varying from knee to ankle, and were sometimes worn with a metal or stiffly ornamented collar.

It is often impossible to find out how garments at this early age were made. Contemporary chroniclers found no space to describe the costumes of the age, and the crudeness of the drawings available and the carelessness of the copyists make many of them of little value.

I O O O—I I O O (*continued*)

This set of drawings shows the fusion of the costume of
the tenth and eleventh centuries. The first figure wears his
braies tight-fitting almost like hose and unbound, with his
buskins, the gauntlet-topped boots covering the ankle.
This fashion is only found between the middle of the eleventh
century and the end of the twelfth. At the bottom of the
page is an example of cross-gartering which was still to be
seen. The motif design on the skirts of this man's tunic is
often seen in contemporary drawings. Any part of the
garment might be embroidered and it was not considered
necessary to maintain the same decorative scheme throughout.
Often the bands of embroidery at the neck, arms, and border
of a tunic are of different designs, and in the tunic illustrated
three distinct designs are used. It is interesting to note,
however, in the illustrations of the time, that the same designs
constantly appear. The embroiderers' lack of originality and
initiative was perhaps compensated by the delicacy and finish
of their work, for which they were renowned on the
Continent.

It is probable that the bands of embroidery lasted many
years and were transferred from one garment to another.
The tasselled tie at the throat of the tunic is an interesting
variation from the usual brooch. The square neck-line
gradually became as popular as the older round style.

I O O O—I I O O (*continued*)

The Danish supremacy had very little immediate effect on costume in England, and to an extent Canute's followers adopted the customs and dress of the English. It is interesting to find, however, that their ideas of cleanliness were in advance of the English. They paid more attention to personal appearance, and they combed their hair at least once a day, bathed once a week and often changed their attire. Although the English looked on these habits as effeminate, their wives and daughters were not slow to approve, and the Danes were popular with the fairer sex.

During the short interval between the Danish and Norman conquests, when the English throne reverted to the Saxon line, there is little to record except the complaint of William of Malmesbury that in the time of Edward the Confessor the English had transformed themselves into Frenchmen and Normans. Edward had spent his life in exile at the Court of Normandy, and it was natural that his sympathies should have been with their manners and customs. William complained that the English not only adopted the Norman strange way of speaking and behaviour, but also their absurdly short tunics, their clipped hair and their mode of hairdressing.

The diagram below indicates how the man's tunic is cut. It will be seen that the top part of the tunic is triangular, with a hole cut out for the head. At a later date the sleeves were even fuller at the base and carried on from the waist itself.

1 0 0 0—1 1 0 0 (*continued*)

For the most part men wore their hair to the tips of the ears with a fringe in front, and although at the Conquest the Normans were closely-cropped and shaved their heads, they soon adopted the English fashion.

Three forms of the Phrygian cap are illustrated on the page facing. With few exceptions this was almost the only type of head-dress worn by men during the eleventh century. Several examples of the simple conical hat illustrated on the opposite page may be found in the Cotton MS. Claudius B IV. This manuscript, which may be seen in the British Museum, well repays study. The colours are brilliant and beautiful and the patterns more varied than in any one manuscript of the period. The drawings themselves, and especially the unfinished ones, have a spontaneity not often found at this early date. Other useful manuscripts in the Cotton collection include the MSS. Tiberius, Caligula, and Cleopatra. The last contains many costumes that are not really of this period, although Cleopatra appears swathed from head to toe in voluminous garments of the eleventh century.

It will be seen that women's heads were still covered and their head-dresses differed hardly at all from those worn several centuries earlier. The last figure has her couvrechef cut with a semicircular front which gives a goffered effect ; another example of this is given on page 41.

I O O O—I I O O (*continued*)

The Norman Conquest had little immediate effect on costume. William of Malmesbury says that the Normans were splendidly dressed, but this refers more to the materials than to the design of their costumes.

When times of peace came hundreds of French craftsmen and domestics came over and settled round the new castles built by the Norman nobles on the land presented to them by the King and round the new churches built by the ecclesiastics from the Continent. Around the Abbey of Battle, for instance, there were Gilbert the Foreigner, Gilbert the Weaver, Benet the Steward, Hugh the Secretary, and Baldwin the Tailor. In the large towns there was a steady influx of traders from France, and all the fineries of the Continent and East, the silks and finely woven materials and personal luxuries, such as gloves and shoes, became available to those who could afford them. Many of these traders had already established business connections with the English in the time of Edward the Confessor, but now they came to settle in earnest, and thus began the slow blending of the conquerors and conquered into one people.

Towards the end of the century, in the reign of William Rufus, the nobles had become wealthy at the expense of the English, and the whole period, not only as regards costume, is one of extravagance. Fashions for the most part remained unaltered, but the materials were costly and decorated to an absurd degree. William of Malmesbury is moved to write " then was the time of flowing locks and extravagant dress, then came in the fashion of shoes with curved points ; then it was the correct thing for young men to outdo women in effeminacy."

The Bayeux Tapestry, believed to have been made at the request of Bishop Odo, half-brother of William I, is an interesting source of information for details of the period, although the exact date of its execution is uncertain. Embroidered in coloured wools on a background of coarse linen, it sets forth in great detail the history of the Conquest. Most of the costumes are naturally military in character, and the English soldiers are shown wearing Norman equipment.

I O O O—I I O O (*continued*)

Men's leg-wear changed considerably during the twelfth century. Loose braies gradually went out of fashion and braies fitting close to the leg were adopted. For centuries the hose had barely reached the knee, but during the first quarter of the century they became longer and often the braies were cut shorter and tucked into the top of the hose. A garment similar to modern shorts was popular in this century. They varied in length, some being like running shorts, with the tunic or shirt tucked into the top, and others much longer and more like the Norfolk breeches worn in the early years of the twentieth century. In all cases the legs were covered, either with the long hose or the tight-fitting braies.

The skirts of the tunic were tucked up in a variety of ways, as illustrated in several of the drawings devoted to this century. Sometimes the hose were rolled down to just above the knee, and it is probable that the band of embroidery at the top of the hose was used as a kind of garter and not merely as an ornament. Men's tunics were worn long and heavily ornamented at this time. The hair and beard were worn long and were carefully combed.

I I OO—I 2 OO

THE first three figures on the page facing are typical costumes of the beginning of the twelfth century. The three at the bottom of the page are all of the eleventh century.

Here may be seen the first example of a woman of high station wearing a train to her gown, the sleeves of which are cut very wide and short and lined with a contrasting colour.

A great change in the appearance of women in this century was in the arrangement of the hair, which is said to be due to Matilda, wife of Henry I. The Queen was an Anglo-Saxon princess, and incidentally it is through her that the present royal family of England is directly descended from Alfred the Great. For over a century women's hair had been concealed beneath head-cloths, and it must have been a welcome relief when the new fashion of displaying the hair was introduced. The hair had previously been plaited in two plaits wound round the head and completely covered by the head-dress. With the appearance of the hair feminine competition begins in earnest, and women outdid each other in the length and thickness of the plaits which now hung down their backs. Artificial hair was introduced, and later the fashion was carried to extremes and the plaits encased in silken cases reached the ground.

Matilda fostered many of the old Anglo-Saxon accomplishments with which ladies of high station had formerly employed themselves, and Norman ladies at the Court followed the Queen's example in spinning, weaving, and embroidery. Some of the ladies worked in their dairies, milking and churning, and the Countess of Chester was famous for her cheese-making.

I I O O—I 2 O O (*continued*)

The figures on the opposite page are taken from a contemporary carving on ivory, and the costumes show the
changes that took place in the early years of the twelfth
century. The woman wears her loose-sleeved gown over the
more tightly fitting under-tunic, the skirt of which is cut
circular so that it falls in a profusion of folds at the bottom.
Bands of embroidery are worn at the waist, the wrists, and
the hem of the outer garment. Women's cloaks are not often
seen fastened together in front at this date, and the method
illustrated in the drawing of fastening the cloak with cords
and tassels became very popular, revealing as it does the
more interesting neck-line of the gown. The veil is semicircular in cut with the straight edge worn at the back and
the curved edge forming a frill on the brow.

The man's costume shows a most interesting innovation
in male attire. The outer or super tunic is the usual Norman
tunic but it is now worn over a full undertunic which reaches
the ground. The wide bands of embroidery on the super-
tunic are typical of the time. Sometimes they are worked
straight, or, as in this case, diagonally; the single band was
more often seen than a repeating design.

The manner of cutting on the circle forms the basis of all
the fullness of garments at this time. It will be noticed that
the man's cloak appears fuller at the front point, and it is
likely that this additional fullness was obtained by cutting
the cloak as illustrated in the sketch below. The two V-
shaped additions to the semicircle give an added grace to
the fullness.

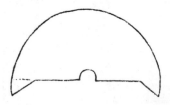

I I O O—I 2 O O (*continued*)

There was a tendency towards individuality in clothes during this century. The long-established forms of arrangement, cut, and shape were no longer strictly adhered to, and the clothes of both men and women began to show signs of personal taste and preference. More originality was displayed in the design of patterns, and sleeves were more varied. The length of the sleeves on the supertunic might be merely a few inches in length and finished with a broad band of embroidery, with the contrasting and tightly-fitting sleeve of the tunic beneath reaching to the wrist, or they might be quite full but fitting to the wrist with a cuff of some contrasting material or embroidery.

From about 1120 women discarded the heavily draped head-veil and a lighter and altogether smaller one took its place. In the case of a lady of quality a coronet was worn over the head-dress.

The mode for longer hair was adopted by the men and carefully combed locks and beards took the place of the short or ear-length cut of the early years of the century. The beards appear to have been dressed with wax of some sort. They were neatly parted and curled in a symmetrical pattern, not unlike the beard-dressing of the Assyrians centuries earlier. The hair was usually cut with a long curled fringe which was plastered down on the forehead in an arrangement of curls, curling outward from the centre. It was worn in ringlets reaching to just below the shoulders, and sometimes it was longer with the ends forming a loose loop of curl. These extremes of fashion and others equally absurd may be seen in contemporary drawings of royal functions and were of course only adopted by the Court. The ordinary man continued to wear his hair cut fairly short all round.

I I O O—I 2 O O (*continued*)

One important change in the appearance of women has already been noted ; another even more important change was the adoption of a close-fitting gown, cut to fit the body tightly down to the hips. Many of these gowns can be seen in the effigies of the period, and they appear to have been worn over a corset of some sort. Few details are available of the exact form this undergarment took, and it is possible that the desired effect of reducing the size of the waist was achieved by a wide band of material or leather sewn tightly round the body. The earliest example in this country of a corset with lacings may be found in an illuminated manuscript of the British Museum, Nero, C.iv, which was completed about 1265. The drawing shows a devil wearing tight-laced corsets, knotted skirts and sleeves and other absurdities of the times.

Yet another change in women's fashions was the new sleeve. Many of these were cut in a bell shape, and others were fairly tight-fitting to the wrist, where a deep band of embroidery formed a gigantic hanging cuff. Towards the end of the century they became so large that they were knotted to save them dragging along the ground. An example of this may be seen on page 57.

The embroidered or otherwise ornamented neckline and the girdle are two other fashions popular at the beginning of the century. Early examples of the girdle were composed of silk and silver and gold threads ornamented with beads. The girdle was worn round the waist, crossed at the back and tied loosely in front below the hips, the tasselled and jewelled ends hanging almost to the hem of the gown.

I I 0 0—I 2 0 0 (*continued*)

Men's belts or girdles assumed a new importance, and many examples show a marked sense of individuality. Previously, belts had served the useful purpose of holding in a loose gown, or carrying the purse, but now they became an object of ornamentation to the super-tunic. They were usually four or five feet in length and made of leather or precious metals. One end was finished with a buckle or a large metal ring and the other tapered and hung down in front of the tunic. The belts worn by the wealthy were costly ; sometimes the whole belt was embroidered or studded with stones and in some examples the ornamentation is confined to the portion near the buckle.

The simple spot patterns of earlier times became less popular as the century advanced. The diaper patterns, those founded on a large chequered ground with a geometrical design within each square, were used extensively throughout the century. Another type of design favoured by the nobility was the large repeating motif between lines or bands of embroidery, examples of which may be found throughout the twelfth and thirteenth centuries. In many contemporary drawings a single motif may be seen embroidered on the garment. It is possible that this was representative of an all-over pattern, as the drawings at this period were so mannered that even furs were represented in heraldic style and everything was simplified in its pictorial representation. The bands of embroidery worn on the garments at this time are represented so stiffly that it is probable that they were set with jewels on a groundwork of fine metal mesh. Even the lighter bands of embroidery have the appearance of stiff tapestry and all of them are enriched with beads or precious stones.

I I 0 0—I 2 0 0 (*continued*)

The drawing from which the illustration on the page facing is taken may be found in the John the Baptist Roll. The colours in this Roll are clear and are beautifully preserved and, what is rare at this time, there is a variety in the clothes depicted. It is interesting to note in most cases the artist seems to have used one model for all the figures depicted.

The parti-coloured super-tunic is one of the earliest examples in existence. The fashion for parti-coloured clothing lasted in varying degrees of popularity from about 1150 until well into the sixteenth century. Sometimes the hose were of the same colour, but more often they were of contrasting colours as illustrated here. It is worthy of note that this is one of the few fashions confined to men, as there are no instances where a woman is seen wearing a parti-coloured gown.

At this time women wore their hair in a variety of ways. Plaits were most popular ; several examples of four plaits may be seen, two worn at the back and two over the shoulders. Sometimes these were bound with silk and not plaited but held together by a complicated method of twisting silken ribands around the tresses.

In the last years of the century the crespine was introduced. This was a net, often of gold mesh, which enclosed the hair. Another new head-dress was the barbette, or band worn under the chin and joined on the top of the head. Introduced by Eleanor, wife of Henry II, it was worn until well into the fourteenth century.

An example of the barbette will be seen at the bottom of page 55, and it is worn with a circular veil over the head and a crown. It will be noticed that there are a great many representations of crowns and coronets in these pages, and it should be remembered that they were worn, as they are still worn on state occasions to-day, by bearers of rank.

I I O O – I 2 O O (*continued*)

Two examples of the girdle or belt are given at the bottom of the page. The first is an interesting arrangement of the knotted girdle worn by a woman. The silken cords are brought through the square buckle and tied in a large knot, and the cord hanging in front is ornamented at intervals with large beads or gems. The second is an example of a man's belt, also with a square buckle. Most belts at this time, however, have circular buckles.

The extensive use of rings as a means of fastening garments at this time even extended to the footwear. On the leg with the dark hose will be seen a boot, with the very full gauntlet top drawn tightly through a ring above the ankle. Boots were far more popular during this century than before and shoes were cut in far greater variety. Long-toed, short-toed, embossed and embroidered, they were sometimes open at the instep but more often closed and reaching well over the ankle. The shoe itself was not often embroidered and separate bands of embroidery were sewn on. Another means of ornamentation was to sew small rings of gold and silver, sometimes even on to the toe and heel of the shoe, and some shoes were covered with fine gold mesh. In some instances gems or beads are sewn on to the gold mesh.

At the top of the page facing is an example of a boot split up the side and laced tightly to fit the leg. Lacing was probably also used for the shorter boot when it was tight-fitting, although few drawings show the details of the fastening.

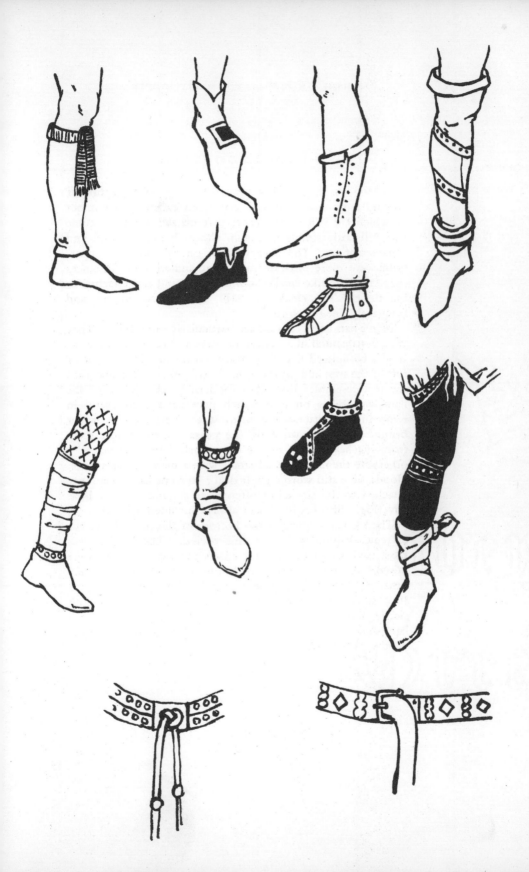

I I O O—I 2 O O (*continued*)

During the last twenty years of the twelfth century it appears from contemporary works, an exceptional number of which are still in existence, that on the whole costume was still fairly simple in design although rich in stuffs and ornamentation. The collars worn on the tunic or super-tunic were more intricate in design, and in some instances they are more like small shoulder capes and not attached to the tunic. The cloak was still semicircular in cut and frequently lined with fur.

Men's hats of this period are particularly interesting. They were ornamented in a variety of ways and often with jewels. It will be noticed that they nearly all finish with a point or tuft at the top, and on those made of soft woollen materials the tuft resembles that on a modern beret. Some of the hats had spikes on top, which may have been useful in removing the hat as the brim was negligible. A wider brimmed hat was worn by the peasantry to protect them from the heat of the sun as they worked in the fields, but otherwise the hats were all small with a mere roll as a brim. Hoods were still worn a great deal ; in some cases they were attached to the cloak but often were a quite separate head covering. Shepherds' cloaks always included a hood.

The woman's gown at the bottom of the page shows the extreme shaping typical of this period. The long sleeves must have swept the ground unless the wearer's arms were raised. A simple contrasting border of material is the only ornament besides the girdle, which is of the plainest design. It is interesting to note that these extremely voluminous sleeves were not adopted by men until a couple of centuries later, and in this case at anyrate the old adage of man aping woman is reversed.

I I O O—I 2 O O (*continued*)

During the twelfth century the Phrygian cap dwindled and degenerated into a caricature of its original form. It is even possible that the curious little cap resembling the cap of an acorn, including its stalk, was a parody of the Phrygian cap. Men's head-dresses can be divided into three groups: the caps already mentioned, the wide-brimmed straw hat of the peasant, and the hood. The brimmed hats were usually conical in shape, and it will be seen from the first head in the second row of drawings that hardly any line occurred where the brim left off and the crown began. A hat consisting of a crown and a brim was not introduced until the following century, and the hat which appears to have a brim at this time was really a hat with the crown elongated so that it gave protection to the eyes and neck.

The hood was worn by all classes, either as a separate item or attached to the tunic, super-tunic, or gown. Following the tendencies of the time, the hoods were usually cut with a slight point at the top.

The three methods of women's hair-dressing illustrated here have all been dealt with. The last is interesting as the earliest example of the crespine or hair-net, and is taken from a panel carved during the last five years of the century. It shows that the hair was worn in " shells " over the ears and not worn in a bun at the back as it was in the following century.

1 1 0 0—1 2 0 0 (*continued*)

During the reign of Stephen from 1135 to 1154 the country was too disturbed by wars and battles for much development in costume, and in the reign of his successor, Henry II, costumes were still plain in design but richer in materials.

Remembering the enmity between the King and Thomas à Becket, it is interesting to find that early in the reign William Fitzstephen says that "never were any two men more absolute friends in Christian times." The King and the Chancellor, as Becket then was, were out riding one day, and seeing a poor man approaching them the King asks if it would not be a real charity to give him a thick warm cloak. Becket replies that it would, and the King should do it. The King jokingly replies that Becket should do so and in friendly jest attempts to pull off the Chancellor's fine new scarlet cloak. Becket resists the attempt, but finally gives way and the poor man receives the cloak.

The popularity of the tight-fitting garments, almost jersey-like in their clinging lines, did not last throughout the century, and they were superseded by more loosely-fitting garments, belted at the waist and often so generously cut that the folds hung over the belt or girdle. This fashion remained in general use until the tight-fitting cotehardie was introduced in the fourteenth century.

The woman's dress illustrated on the opposite page shows traces of both fashions—it is looser but it still retains the clinging lines of earlier years.

I I O O—I 2 O O *(continued)*

Richard I, who came to the throne in 1189, had little
influence on costume. Most of his short reign of ten years
was occupied with the Crusades, and of this time he spent
only eight months in England and his wife Berengaria never
visited the country at all. The King was not slow to take
advantage of his position in raising money for his expedi-
tions. Everything was put up for sale—offices, lordships,
earldoms, shrievalties, castles, towns and estates, and it is
recorded that Bishop Hugh of Durham gave the King a
thousand silver marks to be Justiciar of England and be
excused from the Crusade.

"Let no love of earthly possessions detain you," said
Pope Urban II, exhorting the faithful to free Jerusalem from
the Turks, and although religious fervour undoubtedly
inspired many of the followers of Peter the Hermit in the first
Crusade at the end of the eleventh century and the Crusaders
of the twelfth century, they were a very mixed crowd, and
many of them were out for plunder. The Crusaders who
returned home brought with them the spoils and profits of
battle, including dresses and tunics of brilliant colouring and
Eastern design, and it is interesting to find that the garments
of both men and women at this time show traces of Oriental
influence. Garments were looser and fuller, sleeves wider,
and embroidery more elaborate. In the following century
the influence increased rather than diminished as the century
proceeded.

1200—1300

THERE were no remarkable changes in men's costume in the thirteenth century. A large cloak or mantle with ample sleeves and a variety of caps and hats, often of fantastic shapes, were worn, and are illustrated in the succeeding pages. Women's costume appears to have altered very little during the first part of the century. The long and inconvenient sleeves of the reigns of Henry I and Stephen had gone out of fashion before the accession of John in 1199, and the only addition to feminine apparel appears to have been a garment called a " Pelisson " or pelice, and a chin or neck-cloth called a wimple. King John ordered a grey pelisson with nine bars of fur to be made for the Queen, but apart from the fact that it was a winter garment there are no identifiable examples.

A word may be said here concerning cloaks. The cloaks or mantles worn by the Danes and the Normans in the eleventh century were almost identical, and from contemporary illustrations it is seen that the cloaks of Canute and his wife and William the Conqueror are fastened in a similar manner by cords or laces with tassels. Henry II is said to have introduced a shorter cloak than those previously worn, several examples of which may be seen in the preceding pages. From the latter half of the twelfth century and onwards there is a great variety of cloaks and mantles, and the writers of the times describe them by many different names—the capa, the caputium, the rheno, the super-totus, the balandrana, to mention only a few. It is not possible to trace the distinction between them, and we only know that they were cloaks worn during this period. Many of them were lined with silk or lighter materials for summer wear, and with fur for winter wear, as in the drawing on the opposite page. Those of the wealthy were embroidered and ornamented lavishly.

I 2 0 0—I 3 0 0 *(continued)*

Striped and patterned materials became more popular as the century advanced, and in the drawing of the common soldier at the top of the page facing, not only is his super-tunic striped, but his hose also are ornamented with bands and spots. The sleeves of his garment show the added fullness at the base which often stretched from the waist of the garment to the shoulder. The skirt is split at the front, although in many cases they were split at the sides. Some-times the garments were " dagged," as in the figure at the bottom of the page. One noticeable and lasting effect of the Crusades on fashion was that of shorter cut hair. Long and elaborately curled hair was found to be unsuitable by the Crusaders for their journeys in warmer lands, and thus the shorter mode was introduced and remained the most popular style during the thirteenth century.

Quite early in the century the coif, a close-fitting hat for the head, became popular, and it is possible that this also was introduced by the Crusaders. It was often worn under the head-covering of mail, to protect the head perhaps from the reflected heat of the sun on the mail. In illustrations of the reign of Henry III it is represented white, apparently of linen, and tied under the chin like a child's nightcap. It was worn by all classes, and on the heads of huntsmen, knights in armour, and men in action it has a ludicrous appearance. Most of the costumes on the opposite page are of the middle years of the reign of Henry III.

The shaped but sleeveless gown of the woman on the opposite page is an early example of a fashion which reached the height of its popularity in the following century, and is the forerunner of the cotehardie of the fourteenth and fifteenth centuries.

I 2 0 0—I 3 0 0 (*continued*)

The garment worn by the man in the illustration on the opposite page is taken from an effigy of King John, and shows the Dalmatic, a loose-fitting garment with very wide sleeves, full skirts and belted at the waist. Primarily an ecclesiastical garment, its use was later conceded to emperors and kings at their coronation and when assisting at High Mass. In the account of John's coronation robes it is mentioned as being of a dark purple colour. The stiff gold collar is heavily ornamented with jewels of so large a size that one would doubt their reality if it were not for jewels of a similar nature still reposing in the treasuries of several cathedrals on the Continent and which at one time ornamented priestly vestments. The precious stones mostly used in this century include topazes of almost unbelievable size, emeralds, garnets, sapphires, rubies, diamonds, amethysts, amber, and rock crystal.

John was extravagant in dress but he introduced no new styles or fashions and was content to wear the designs of the previous century, but decorated in a costly or showy manner.

Gloves were an important part of a king's dress, and it will be noticed that in the illustration the back of the King's glove, which was probably made of kid or calfskin, is studded with a precious stone. Gloves do not appear to have been worn in England before the beginning of the eleventh century, and it is interesting to note that no gloves are visible in the Bayeux Tapestry, not even on the hands of Harold, who in one section is seen carrying a hawk. The early gloves were bag-shaped, and gloves with fingers were not introduced until the twelfth century. One of the earliest examples of this kind is seen on an effigy of Henry II.

1 2 0 0 — 1 3 0 0 *(continued)*

Mention has not yet been made of a garment first introduced by the Crusaders in the twelfth century as a part of
military attire, but which later achieved wider popularity
and became a part of civil attire.   This garment was the
surcoat or surcote, and in many respects it resembled the
super-tunic, and indeed is often referred to as such.   Its
main purpose was to protect the armour of the Crusaders
from the weather, from the rain as one authority asserts,
but more probably from the rays of the Syrian sun which
heated it excessively.   This surcoat descended in folds to
the knee, was without sleeves and usually open at the front
or sides.   A soldier at the top of page 87 is wearing one of
this type over his hauberk or coat of mail.   The surcoats
sometimes had the distinguishing red cross, but often the
heraldic device of a noble.   The surcoat is also the name
given to a garment worn over the tight-fitting garment or
cote worn by women which superseded the tunic during part
of this century.   The super-tunic was the garment worn by
both sexes over another tunic, and is to be seen in great
variety in this century.   Sometimes they were knee-length,
but often almost as long as the under-tunic ; they were
worn full and otherwise, with openings at the sides or front.
The sleeves vary in length and design.

An interesting garment is illustrated at the bottom of
the page facing.   It was an outer garment, loosely fitting and
unbelted, hanging from the shoulder to the calf or ankle and
with very full sleeves.   The sleeves were slit at the elbow
so that the hand might come out, and sometimes this slit
extended almost to the end of the sleeve.   These garments
were lined with a contrasting material and sometimes worn
with a hood attached.   Another example is illustrated on
page 69, and in this case the garment has a large fur collar
cut to fit tightly over the shoulder.

1 2 0 0—1 3 0 0 (*continued*)

The long reign of Henry III, from 1216 until 1272, is referred to by historians as a period of extravagance, but it will be seen from the preceding pages of drawings and in those which follow that as far as the form of costume is concerned it is not so, and extravagance is confined to the materials used and to ornamentation.

Many and rare costly materials were used at this time. Damask, a rich description of figured satin or linen, received its name from the city of Damascus where it was presumably first manufactured. In a romance of the period, *The Squire of Low Degree*, there is a reference to it :

> Damask white and azure blewe,
> Well diapered with lillies new.

Velvet, or vellet as it is sometimes referred to in the thirteenth century, was occasionally used for garments, including the mantles of the Knights Templars. Another material used was baldekin or baudekyn, a costly stuff of silk and gold, so called because it was originally manufactured at Baldech, one of the names of Babylon or Baghdad. It was used for robes of state, canopies and curtains, and Matthew Paris speaks of it in 1247 as forming part of the royal vestments of Henry III when he conferred the honour of knighthood on William de Valence.

Other materials used were samite, a stuff wholly of silk, but frequently interwoven with gold and silver and embroidered in a lavish manner ; cendal, a silken stuff used not only for garments but for flags, horse-trappings, and curtains. The celebrated banner of St. Denis is said to have been made of " cendal pur." Tissue and cloths of gold and silver were also much used, and silk had become quite common and was used extensively.

1 2 0 0—1 3 0 0 *(continued)*

The next page of drawings has been devoted to the costumes worn by the poorer classes in this century. The first figure is wearing a loose tunic over a shirt and what may be described as breeches or drawers. They were probably split at the sides as in the figure beneath, and for convenience the ends were knotted together. The third figure shows the tunic gathered up at the waist, and similar examples are to be found in the two previous centuries. It is not clear how this was done, unless the folds were tucked into the belt worn beneath.

The old man with the stick is wearing a hood with a loose cape. Countrywomen wore long loose gowns with or without a simple girdle. The villages were self-supporting and the peasants spun their own coarse cloth from wool and hemp. The natural wool-coloured garments were often dyed with natural dyes—bright blues, reds and greens.

Many of the peasants went barefoot when working in wet or marshy land, but at times wore shoes made of rough tanned leather or black cloth.

1 2 0 0—1 3 0 0 (*continued*)

The crespine, the net for confining the hair, has already been described, and several examples are given in the preceding pages. The barbette, to which reference has also been made, the crespine and the fillet were the three main factors in head-dresses. The fillet was the band worn round the head and was usually made of stiff linen varying in width from one and a half to three inches. It was always worn with either the crespine or barbette and more often both. Sometimes the upper edge was serrated, sometimes goffered or cut in points. It was not always composed of net, and sometimes a plain material was used to tuck away the hair. The hair was worn either plaited or loose or even tied into a large loose bun at the back.

A flat-topped bonnet something like a pill-box in shape was introduced soon after Henry III came to the throne. The illustrations on the page facing show the variety of ways in which these head-dresses were worn. On the third head, instead of the more usual fillet, the barbette is worn with a veil wound round the head. The head immediately beneath it shows a useful way of disposing of the veil when working. It is loosely wound round the head and tied in front, giving a turban-like effect.

I 2 O O—I ʒ O O (*continued*)

The first figure on the page facing represents a common soldier of the time donning his coat of mail, and although armour is not included within the scope of this book, a few examples have been inserted to show how the coats of mail were connected with the other garments worn in the thirteenth century. In this case the tunic, tight-sleeved but full-skirted, is split at the front to give as much play and freedom as possible. Independent thigh coverings were worn over the hose and tied to the waist in the same manner as the hose. The coif is worn under the metal head-covering.

The next figure shows a countrywoman with her gown split at the sides like an apron and showing an undertunic beneath. By this time gloves were worn for rough work in the fields. The two women's gowns at the bottom of the page are earlier examples of the garment described on page 78 ; in both cases the sleeves are attached to the shoulder so that they may be worn in either of the ways depicted. The method of tying the sleeves in a knot behind was easier than rolling the sleeves back from the wrist, as in most cases the sleeves were tight-fitting. One of the women is wearing striped hose, a fashion only rarely adopted by women.

The pouch hanging from the waist of the other woman is interesting. It is closed at the top by means of two cords and is covered with a fine mesh work, the bottom being ornamented with beads. Another example will be found on page 65.

All the drawings on the opposite page are taken from the Bible Moralise, one of the most interesting and informative illuminated manuscripts of the thirteenth century. It is a particularly valuable record of costume of about 1260 or a little later, as it shows not only the clothes of royalty and the nobility, but of every class, including peasants and the common soldiers.

1200—1300 (*continued*)

The two costumes on the page facing show a milkmaid and shepherd of the middle of the thirteenth century. The milkmaid is far from being poorly clad ; her dress is simple though quite in accordance with the prevailing fashions, and her cloak is lined with a contrasting colour. Her headdress is of the approved mode, but her hair is not confined in a crespine, being loosely knotted at the back. There is little difference between her attire and that of the ladies at the bottom of the following page of illustrations, and only the milk pail indicates her calling.

The dress of her companion, on the other hand, is nothing like the garments worn by his master. The short but full tunic is well adapted to his work, and his hood with the sheepskin cape attached, although picturesque is strictly utilitarian. The highcut shoes and the leg-bindings hardly differ from those worn centuries earlier. The working man of the thirteenth century is not often seen wearing hose, either his legs are covered with braies or short hose or bound with leather, and usually he went barefoot.

1 2 0 0—1 3 0 0 (*continued*)

The second figure illustrated on the opposite page is wearing a garment similar to those worn by the women at the bottom of page 75. It was worn fairly short, and in this instance is split at the front and has no belt or girdle. Pelice is the Norman-French word for fur, and fur-lined gowns of many varieties are referred to as pelissons. Fur was used a great deal at this time both for lining and trimming. Among the furs used were ermine, sable, squirrel, marten, minevair, which was probably pure white ermine without tails or spots and very costly, and vair, which seems to have been a composite fur available in several forms. The fur of a species of squirrel or weasel, which was grey on the back and white on the throat and belly, was also called vair.

Although the tunic of the last figure on the page is simple and of the usual cut, the collar and cuff strike a new note in decoration. In the manuscript from which it is taken they are both represented in gold. It is possible that they were made of leather painted gold, or even cloth of gold, although its use was usually confined to dresses for state and ceremonial occasions. The use of gold leaf is so lavish in manuscripts at this time that the artist may have erred on the side of accuracy in the interests of pictorial decoration.

I 2 O O—I 3 O O *(continued)*

The grotesque exaggeration of the barbette and fillet at the bottom of the page is taken from an illustration which represents the hair encased in a sort of green bag. The fillet is a gem-studded coronet. This lady's cloak is fastened in an interesting manner, as the cord which holds the two sides together has ornamented buckles, one of which is adjustable, and thus permitting the cloak to be worn in a variety of ways. The next figure shows the plaits encased in long silken tubes bound or ornamented with gold or silver cord. The three little beaded tassels at the ends of the tubes are often seen in examples of this fashion. After about the middle of the century the fashion for plaits was largely superseded by the fillet and crespine. The crespine was worn in a variety of ways and made of many different materials, from those made of gold or silver net and studded with jewels worn by the wealthy and descending in splendour to the plain linen or net covering worn by countrywomen. In some cases the hair within was worn at the sides, but often it was worn at the back.

I 2 0 0—I 3 0 0 (*continued*)

When Edward I came to the throne in 1272, the fashions of Henry III's reign remained unaltered, except that garments became even simpler. Queen Eleanor followed her husband's example, and the costumes of this reign are the simplest in the history of this country. But although the clothes were so simple they were dignified and graceful, especially cloaks, which were worn in a variety of ways. Unnecessary trimmings and ornaments were abandoned, but costly materials were still used, and it is recorded that a hundred lords and ladies " clad all in silk " sat at the Round Table at Kenilworth. It was the King's aim to be the model of the fashionable French notions of chivalry of the time, and one of his attempts was to renew the faded glories of the Court of King Arthur.

Gowns were cut full and long and hung in folds at the feet, and, as will be noticed in the woman's gown at the bottom of the opposite page, girdles were not worn. Towards the end of the century the skirt of the outer gown is so ample as to form a train, and it is interesting to read that this fashion was condemned by the moralists of the time. Robert de Brunne in his *Handlyng Sinne* writes of the wickedness of wearing trains, and tells at length the story of how two monks saw a woman with a devil sitting on the end of her train.

I 2 O O—I 3 O O *(continued)*

Men's head-dresses continue in great variety, and it will be seen in the drawings on the opposite page that several of them show the influence of the East. The hats with the turned-up brims appear fairly frequently in the second half of the century and were made of felt or cloth.

During the reign of Edward I the hood began to develop in a curious fashion. The peak of the hood grew longer, and by the end of the reign it was often three feet in length. Its subsequent development is described and illustrated in a companion book to the present volume which deals with the costume of the Later Middle Ages.

The popularity of the coif, the tight-fitting bonnet illustrated in the last drawing, remained undiminished. It is interesting to find that in the reign of Henry III priests were forbidden to wear the coif except when travelling, as it was alleged that the disguise it afforded often resulted in priests forgetting their priestly functions.

Many men at this time followed the French fashion of being clean-shaven. Beards and moustaches were still worn, however, and received careful attention.

I 2 OO—I 3 OO (*continued*)

It will be seen from the drawings on the page facing that often the whole body, from head to foot and the tips of the fingers, was encased in armour of some form or other. Over the hauberk, or coat of mail, was worn a surcoat, which in the twelfth century was quite plain or embroidered with gold or silver, but in the thirteenth century became more elaborate and ornamented with heraldic devices. A belt, often richly ornamented, was worn round the waist and from it hung the sword. The sleeves of the hauberk usually extended beyond the wrist and covered the hands, which could be slipped out, however, through an oval opening corresponding to the palm. The hauberk was also constructed with a hood or coif of mail attached, which could be drawn over the head or flung back over the shoulders.

The conical steel cap with the nose guard, illustrated at the bottom of the page, was the common head-piece of the two previous centuries. The first figure shows the improved head-piece which encloses all the head, except the face, which was defended by a vizor.

English Costume of the Later Middle Ages

The Fourteenth & Fifteenth Centuries

Drawn and Described by Iris Brooke

Eight illustrations in colour and thirty-two in black-and-white

Uniform with this book

THIS volume covers the Fourteenth and Fifteenth Centuries, and is copiously and charmingly illustrated.[1] Throughout these two centuries the main lines of costume were little changed, and they were generally of an elegance and beauty that has never been surpassed in England; but within this frame there was an astonishing variety of detail.[2]

The period is one of the most fascinating but also one of the most difficult in the history of costume, and only those who have themselves made some study of the subject will realise just how much hard work has gone to the making of these apparently effortless drawings. The Fourteenth and Fifteenth centuries run riot in the exaggeration, the variety, the beauty and the absurdity of their fashions. It is not too much to say that Miss Brooke, while indulging us with a wealth of detail, develops her pictorial narrative with such skill and such a good sense of direction that difficulties vanish, and we are left with a clear yet comprehensive impression.[3]

[1] *The London Mercury.*   [2] *The Parthenon.*   [3] *The Times.*

A. & C. BLACK, LTD., 4, 5 & 6 SOHO SQUARE, LONDON, W.1

English Costume in the Age of Elizabeth

The Sixteenth Century

Drawn and Described by Iris Brooke

Eight illustrations in colour and thirty-two in black-and-white

Uniform with this book

THIS book covers the whole of the Sixteenth Century, and the progress of fashion during that period from simplicity to fantastic extravagance;[1] there is grace and delicacy; there is variety and humanity. The costumes are wonderful and the people who wear them are human.[2]

Miss Brooke has carried out a difficult task with much skill. The extravagancies and fantastic trimmings of the Elizabethan dandies are almost a byword. To choose the representative styles when all was so inherently complex and when the competition to own exotic and fanciful garments was so fierce, calls for no small power of discrimination.[3] Miss Brooke's drawings, in line or colour, are simple and clear. She is never tedious or long-winded, and her book is a good companion for the more staid text-books of history.[1] Her interesting quotations from contemporary sources make the book a very human and convincing survey.[4]

The book will be useful to artists, stage designers, and writers; it is beautifully produced, and in addition to its utility is a delightful possession.[5]

[1] *Morning Post.*   [2] *Cambridge Review.*   [3] *The Antique Collector.*
[4] *The Schoolmaster.*   [5] *New Britain.*

A. & C. BLACK, LTD., 4, 5 & 6 SOHO SQUARE, LONDON, W.1.

English Costume of the Seventeenth Century

Drawn and Described by Iris Brooke

Eight illustrations in colour and thirty-two in black-and-white

Uniform with this book

A N extraordinarily interesting and varied century for costume. Miss Brooke's vigorous drawings give an extremely good idea of the way in which Jacobean clothing, taking over Elizabethan stiffness, gradually evolves a distinctive formality of its own.

Miss Brooke's instinct for selection and omission is admirable,[1] her work is accurate, both in text and illustration.[2] She has made a careful selection from a bewildering wealth of material, and has so arranged her illustrations that every phase in the development of seventeenth-century costume can be easily and quickly looked up.[3] This, coupled with the racy descriptions and extracts from what contemporaries have to say about the fashions, make it a source of entertainment as well as a useful guide to the dress of the period.[4]

This is a book which any lady will receive with delight; dramatists will turn to it with profit, antiquaries with curious interest, and historians for the study of Jacobean and Carolinean social life.[5]

[1] *The Times.*   [2] *Glasgow Herald,*   [3] *The Amateur Theatre.*
[4] *The Connoisseur.*   [5] *Record.*

A. & C. BLACK, LTD., 4, 5 & 6 SOHO SQUARE, LONDON, W.1.

English Costume of the Eighteenth Century

Drawn by Iris Brooke
Described by James Laver

Eight illustrations in colour and thirty-two in black-and-white

Uniform with this book

Another volume in this admirable series can only be noted with gratitude.[1] It is a thoroughly practical book, and as instructive as it is pleasing. The selective ease with which both designer and commentator have threaded their ways through the intricacy of costume-detail compels admiration. The subject is apt to lead its enthusiasts into length and dullness; but without any sacrifice of plan, accuracy, or perspective, Miss Brooke and Mr. Laver have packed their comprehensive survey into some eighty pages, enlivened by a pretty wit, and governed by a nice feeling for essentials in word and line.

Besides being invaluable to students of costume, the book will delight the ordinary reader. It is no easy task for the expert to satisfy them both at the same time; and the collaborators are to be congratulated on their achievement.[2] Perhaps the collaborators should be counted as three, not two, for author and illustrator owe much to the way in which the publishers have produced the book in a manner so perfectly in keeping with the spirit of the text and pictures.[3]

[1] *The Oxford Magazine.*   [2] *The Times.*   [3] *Drama.*

A. & C. BLACK, LTD., 4, 5 & 6 SOHO SQUARE, LONDON, W.1.

English Costume of the Nineteenth Century

Drawn by Iris Brooke

Described by James Laver

Twelve illustrations in colour and thirty in black-and-white

Uniform with this book

Iɴ a slim and elegant volume Mr. James Laver has described the changing fashions of the last century simply and briefly, and Miss Iris Brooke, with her delicate and accurate illustrations, has made the simpering modes and manners of an affected age come blushingly to life.[1] The text is scholarly and sly, as is desirable; the numerous illustrations are clear, accurate, and often witty.[2]

Miss Brooke has most successfully recaptured the air and the style of the contemporary fashion plates, and her groups are in themselves witty commentaries on the manners as well as the costumes of the times.[3] They have grace and delicacy, and are entirely free from flamboyance and caricature.[4]

This is a very practical book for actors and artists and anyone who needs reliable information on the costume of the period;[5] but it would be entirely wrong to give the impression that it is only a book for the theatrical designer. It will delight anybody with a sense of period who cares for a book with a thoroughly individual flavour, published at a ridiculously low price,[6] so beautifully produced that it will attract everyone into whose hands it comes.[7]

[1] *The Saturday Review.* [2] *The Oxford Magazine.* [3] *The Burlington Magazine.* [4] *The Era.* [5] *Vogue.* [6] *Drama.* [7] *Everyman.*

A. & C. BLACK, LTD., 4, 5 & 6 SOHO SQUARE, LONDON, W.1.

English Children's Costume

Since 1775

Drawn and Described by Iris Brooke
Introduction by James Laver

Eight illustrations in colour and thirty-two in monochrome

Uniform with this book

THE same agreeable collaboration.[1] Miss Iris Brooke has followed up her successful *English Costume of the Nineteenth Century* by an equally attractive book on English Children's Costume, to which Mr. James Laver has written a delightful introduction.[2]

Miss Brooke's clear, gay drawings and pithy descriptions of the garments inflicted upon the young and innocent from 1775 up till a year or two ago make a very delightful, instructive, and useful little book . . . a fearful and fascinating pictorial record of juvenile fashions which it is well worth our while to ponder and impossible not to enjoy.[3] Mr. James Laver speculates in an interesting and witty fashion upon the tendency to make the dress of adults of both sexes like the dress of children, and upon the quicker reaction to outside influences discernible in children's fashions than in those of their elders.[4]

Deep thinkers will find plenty of material here ; less serious-minded persons can read, look, and be amused.[5] The costumier, artist, and producer of plays will find it of considerable value. Useful for those who have to consider period dresses,[6] it is a wholly charming book, and I can think of few who would not like to possess it for one reason or another.[7]

[1] *The Observer.* [2] *The Spectator.* [3] *The Times.* [4] *The Scotsman.*
[5] *Oxford Magazine.* [6] *Tailor and Cutter.* [7] *Manchester Guardian.*

A. & C. BLACK, LTD., 4, 5 & 6 SOHO SQUARE, LONDON, W.1.

PRINTED BY MORRISON AND GIBB LTD., LONDON AND EDINBURGH